How to Read a Civil War Letter

by Gregory R. Jones, Ph.D.

Copyright © 2015 by Gregory R. Jones

Cover image credit: *Ohio University's Mahn Center, Athens, Ohio. Brown Family Collection Box 2, Folder 112.*
Cover design: Gregory R. Jones

Table of Contents

Introduction

     Correspondence between soldiers and their associates back home provides a wonderful lens of the Civil War world. This book will help readers learn how to go about the process of reading and making sense of those invaluable resources. The title of this work is not complicated and neither are its instructions, but there are many people who can benefit from learning the methods presented herein. For scholars, genealogists, history buffs, and the generally curious, the context clues and format of 19th century writing might be a bit difficult to discern. As I embarked on my own dissertation work, reading nearly eight hundred Civil War letters on my own, I realized that no one had quite chronicled a good way to go about the process. I had been taught how to read political speeches, newspapers, and even personal diaries, but no one had taught me the intricacies of nineteenth century correspondence. So here is the book I wish I had.

     What I learned in the process of reading those letters is that there were and remain very clear patterns of correspondence. Think about how you might contact a loved one today; first you give an update on health, then a summary of what you have done since the last time you communicated, and then perhaps an inquiry into the other person's well being. To a large extent, 19th century Americans followed that same kind of formula. But they also used a lot of different formalities that folks in the 21st century would not use.

Examples of exceedingly formal writing include the use of titles for loved ones and family members. Writers referred to specific events with very clear titles, expressed emotions with detachment, and often expected the letter to be read by outsiders. And this fact is precisely the key in developing an understanding of any Civil War letter. It is imperative that the reader know the intended audience. Of course no Civil War soldier sat down to write his correspondence with historians or genealogists in mind. Rather, these individuals were focused on the letter's addressee. However, they were also interested in informing many folks beyond the addressee such as the rest of the family and potentially the entire home front community. Sometimes soldiers even included in-text cues about who the message was for. "Tell the children I love them" was a clear cue for a message to be read aloud. Other times the writer would specifically write *not* to let anyone else read a particularly intimate passage, often expressing deep homesickness or financial concerns deemed to be too personal for a broader readership.

Speaking of intended audience, this book is meant to help individuals who may have little desire to pursue formal training as a historian, but are lucky enough to have access to primary source Civil War letters. Maybe they were a distant relative's handwritten letters found in grandma's attic, a collection found at the local historical society, or even scanned sources freely available online, but to make sense of them most readers need a tool to orient oneself to the war, the era, and the means of correspondence.

The format of the book is simple. It provides four chapters each with a practical, instructive purpose. There is very little theory presented here. Rather, it is a straightforward process-oriented book. That said, each letter is different. For the sake of clarity, the book focuses largely on letters written in English to personal connections. Letters written in other languages (which are many, especially in German) will necessitate translation. Depending upon the purpose of the overall research project, it may be necessary to pay an expert to do the translation. Just like 19th century English is not quite the same as that of the 21st century, it may even be best to find a translator who can specialize in historic foreign language. Letters written in military and political contexts can be even more loaded with imagery not covered in this book. The vast majority of Civil War correspondence available for research is personal in nature, so that is the focus of this guide.

Before assuming that readers of this guide already have letters to read, it is important to discuss how to go about gaining access to letters. Published letters are readily available both on the Internet and in published book collections. They are relatively easy to find, but also often have their own interpretations by professional historians. If a researcher wants to find unique, previously unread or seldom read Civil War letters there are a few places to look: the National Archives and Records Administration, state archives, local or county historical societies, and private collections. Some are easier to locate and access than others. Some places only allow access to sources from experienced researchers. Others may charge a fee for entry or duplication, but more on that later.

Probably the easiest way for an ordinary person to access these kinds of sources is through the local historical society or local library. Typically local archivists have access to these sources. Some archives have more sources than they can possibly transcribe, so volumes and volumes of letters sit in acid-free boxes just awaiting transcription. Because most historical societies are grossly understaffed and underfunded, they find themselves in need of volunteer assistance with these types of sources. So if you find yourself as a historical society volunteer reading this book, you have come to the right place for assistance.

In the context of a professional archive setting, the first step is obviously to request to see a letter or collection of letters. After requesting to see a letter, usually the archivist brings the letter to the researcher. At that moment the letter holds millions of possibilities. It may hold secrets that no other document has ever taught us. It may be a letter you have read before and did not realize it. But most importantly, the letter holds its own message in multiple layers that have to be teased out, listened to, and understood. In order to get at those layers of text and subtext, a trained eye looks for more than the words on the page. And that first magical read may be the most exciting. Every read after that first time through results in more analysis and less emotional attachment. After discerning that the letter is worthy for your project or helpful in some way, get a copy made and take it home for further study.

The initial read through, though, may be the most influential in determining your next steps. Take a few notes as soon as you finish that first reading.

How did it make you feel? Who does it seem to be written to and from (even if you cannot make out the names perfectly)? When was it written? Did it seem like the writer was sad or happy? Did it have a sense of adventure or a sense of loss? There are a wide range of emotional states present throughout the Civil War. One common mistake made by amateur historians is to assume the context of the source before reading for further context clues. Historians sometimes assume that President Lincoln was in the same mental and emotional state throughout the entire war, but of course he was not. With the benefit of hindsight historians have come to understand the death of his son Willie as a crucial moment in his life and presidency which influenced the way he coped with Civil War casualties. This one moment of context changes our understanding of several other sources. So when embarking on a journey to understand a new soldier or a new source, try not to assume too much about the context on the initial read through. Let the source hit you with whatever energy, emotion, and power that it has to offer. There will be time for contextualization, analysis, and even a bit of cynicism in later stages.

One of the immediate hurdles that amateur historians face is a fear that they might "mess it up" or "get it wrong." Abolish this fear immediately. No historical thinker, professional or not, has a monopoly on accurate historical thinking and there are always thousands of ways to interpret a document. The best approach is to be willing to learn from the source. It is not something to wedge into your project, exhibit, or dissertation. It is a piece of history that shows the connection between people who lived many years ago. Taking a moment to understand those people, who they were and what they did, goes a long way in analyzing the document. But having a right attitude at the start can do great things for work later in the process. Take a deep breath, read, and write down what jumps off the page.

Chapter 1: Making Sense of 19th Century Writing

As mentioned in the introduction, nineteenth century writing followed a formula that feels very intuitive to humans in the 21st century as well. It is a practical structure that provides great information for the reader. It also is laid out nicely in nearly every letter, allowing the reader to know what cues to look for in further understanding the ideas presented in the note. Most letters have the following content: routing information (who it is from, who it is to), greeting, personal update, discussion of regional and national news, inquiries, and salutation. That sounds awfully easy to follow. Here are some of the things that complicate that formula: unclear titles of writer and recipient, incorrect identifying information, cross-thatch writing (that significantly deters comprehension), tiny writing, illegible writing, use of nicknames and unclear phrases, and uncertainty who actually authored the note. This chapter serves as a way to help letter readers make sense of these various structural and logistical issues in 19th century writing.

Routing Information (who it is from, who it is to)

Routing information is about more than the author and recipient's addresses. In the case of Civil

War letters, routing information may be full of integral context clues. It often will include some of the military detail for further reference. However, abbreviations for military units were not consistent. For example, an address might read "Sixty-Third Ohio Volunteer Infantry" on one note, or "63rd OVI" on another note, or later in the war might merely say "63 OVVI." The extra "V" in this case denotes "veteran," but there are many different variations that may involve finding context in the letter itself, doing research on the structure of the army the soldier served in, or even consulting an outside military history specialist. Unfortunately there is not one comprehensive place to locate all military information from the Civil War, largely because most units were part of a state infrastructure rather than federal. When searching for details on a particular unit designation, be sure to consult state-level resources for best accuracy.

Often times soldiers included their rank and unit, but not a location. Those of us born in the post-WWII era see this as some sort of covert masking of location, but in the pre-radio era when it took several days or weeks for letters to arrive, that information was probably not terribly secret. Rather, soldiers put this ambiguous address on letters because they were unsure where they would be from day to day or even hour to hour. Writing the unit designation would ensure that the mail arrived to them even if they were several states away by the time the recipient responded. It is important to remember that these were intelligent, problem-solving people who relied upon letters for all of their personal updates. Getting that information right was of utmost concern to them, so they would not have left it vague without good reason.

As for the home front recipients, sometimes the location seems vague to 21st century eyes, often nothing more than a name and a town. Remember that local post offices were linked to townships and smaller governmental structures. There were no massive housing plans of suburban sprawl necessitating address detail. It is quite possible that there really was only one "Brown family" in some regional Ohio post offices. This, again, is an instance when readers and researchers have to be patient with the document.

But it is quite possible that the reader can get out of the routing information enough to know who the main characters are. From that point details like rank, relationship, and affiliation might become further clear through the early marks of the letter itself. Keep an eye out for a date pretty much anywhere on the document, including on the envelope or at the top (near the routing information). Civil War era writers used a variety of styles for date, including full written-out formal dates and myriad abbreviations. Also note that there can sometimes be inaccuracies in that information, but that will be covered in depth later.

Greeting

The greeting of a nineteenth century letter often does not seem particularly complicated. Often times it involves the word "Dear" followed by a first name. However, sometimes greetings are a bit more complicated, including formality that may seem unnecessary given the parties involved. For example, if someone in the 21st century were to write to an aunt or uncle, they might use "Dear Aunt Sue," as a greeting. However, in the 19th century that same letter might be addressed, "Dear Mrs. Susan Jones," even though it seems overly formal to readers today. Nineteenth century writers often utilized titles of formality, even among close friends and family. Sometimes families included the rank of the soldier they wrote to, even if he was their loved one. There are primarily two reasons for this formality. The first is that the 19th century world had a greater sense of respect and honor. Showing deference to a person, even within one's own family, was part of a culture that was far more formal than the 21st century.

Secondly, most writers assumed that their letters were not fully private. Writing with a formal greeting would allow potential interlopers with the exact intended audience of the letter.

Greetings sometimes give an indication of the intended tone of a letter. So, for example, a letter written to family intended to stay within the family might have a more informal tone from the start. But a letter intended to be read to the entire family or even the community would be a bit more formal. These cues can be found in the use of pet names or formal titles. Similarly, if you happen to run across a full collection from a particular writer, there may be patterns in greetings. As another example, there once was a set of correspondence between two lovers including the greeting "Dear Ed," in many of the letters. After their mid-war breakup, the writer used the far colder "Dear Mr. Brown," as her greeting in subsequent correspondence. That one change communicated more than several sentences of the letter itself. These kinds of cues are invaluable to deeper levels of interpretation.

Personal Update

Writers provided personal updates covering a wide range of details. Where some letter writers went into considerable depth, others barely discussed themselves. This is a way in which the reader can discern a bit about the personality of the letter writer. But the personal update often included information about personal health, location or status, and a rudimentary discussion of the writer in relationship to the recipient.

The personal health section often included self diagnoses of potential injuries or diseases. Many Civil War soldiers struggled with health issues. While in the 21st century it might be difficult to grasp writing a letter about a personal affliction, it is important to remember these letters were the primary mode of communication. Letter writers sometimes gave lurid detail about various illnesses. But more often than not the health update had only minor problems with sore feet, hunger, or overall fatigue. When soldiers had major illnesses, someone else had to pen the letter for them.

Soldiers spent a considerable amount of time regaling movement and locations. Sometimes they would write with great focus about the surrounding area. Soldiers often compared the unique landscapes to home and to other locations visited. Soldiers also spent substantial time describing elements of the landscape to assist readers in visualizing the location. Those same soldiers often spent several lines describing camp, especially if it was a location they expected to stay for a long time.

Letter writers were concerned with maintaining relationships with the people at home, so part of the update included reinforcing the relationship with the letter's recipient. This sometimes included reassurances of love, assurance of fidelity and or sobriety, and in the case of children, sometimes included directives to behave or listen to their mother. These sorts of reinforcements of the relationship are in nearly every Civil War letter. They do more than just report news or the state of things. They are sure to personalize and reaffirm the relationships that still existed, if even from afar. Sometimes as a part of this section the letter writer would essentially demand that the recipient write more often, more consistently, or even longer letters. Soldiers clearly craved greater connection with the folks at home.

Discussion of Regional and National News

The discussion of regional and national news was present in many of the letters from the Civil War as soldiers were starved for information. They were constantly hearing rumors that they wanted to have confirmed. Nearly every month of the war there was a rumor that the war might end any day for a thousand different reasons. With such promise of a trip home, the end of war, or even bad news from the home front, soldiers constantly sought confirmation of that kind of news.

Regional news was particularly important. While some soldiers could rely on getting a major newspaper that could cover their region, many soldiers waited for loved ones to forward on copies of the local town newspaper. These types of regional updates were important for maintaining soldiers' ties to the home front. Yet these types of news also helped to frustrate and upset soldiers, who found stories of unrest at home or pending attack on their homes to be excruciating. Likewise, national news often served to upset soldiers who felt powerless in the midst of the grand narrative. Soldiers wrote of speculation and theories regarding politics, military news, and of course the developments of the war itself. Not all soldiers participated in such banter and speculation, but many spent several pages per week postulating about the national state of affairs, whether the war would end, and what should really happen to "those abolitionists," or "those traitors."

Inquiries

One of the most important sections in each letter were the inquiries to the letter's recipient. Regardless of who the letter was sent to, the letter writer almost always asked questions. When writing to their wives or mothers at home, soldiers often asked for detail on the home itself. How were the animals? How was the farm? How are the kids? What sermon did you hear on Sunday? How are you feeling? These types of inquiries were extremely common, often prompting the letter recipient both to write back and to structure a response with a personal update involved. Sometimes letter writers asked questions that were a bit more difficult to answer, but often they were the kind of ordinary questions most folks ask of a loved one today.

Salutation

Much like the greeting, the salutation could carry volumes of unwritten meaning. Because letter writers were not always sure how much they might write in a given letter or how much time they'd have to complete it, sometimes salutations were written with a rush. Instead of the greeting, often written with considerable time to think and plan, oftentimes salutations were composed in a rush with the mail heading out or in order to complete some other task. Soldiers sometimes signed letters with pet names, abbreviations, or no name at all. Perhaps equally strange, many times soldiers signed their letters with a full name, rank, and location for the same reasons that they did so for the greeting; they wanted to ensure that any return mail could make it to them.

This formulaic structure appeared in letter after letter, north and south, early war and late. Many of the structural components are present in every conversation or update as inherent human communication. But yet there were other elements clearly embedded in the context of Civil War. As contemporary readers embark on the task of determining layers of meaning in a Civil War letter, it is important to consider where soldiers were, who else might be reading their letters, and how often they were able to communicate with home. Some soldiers could send letters daily. Others were so deep into enemy territory or a part of such an unreliable post system that their letters may not arrive for weeks on end. Allowing these kinds of logistical and practical details to inform analysis will make for a stronger read and better takeaway points.

As I entered into my own research on the Civil War, I wanted to be sure to account for this type of background information and quickly learned that there was no universal constant. It was not evident the connections between education, background, region, or literacy to how a letter appeared. One particularly difficult situation I had to deal with was a young lady by the name of Emma Hudgel. She was courting a soldier by the name of Edwin Brown. In fact, their romance, as it ebbed and flowed throughout the war, was one of the more interesting human interest stories I discovered in my research. But Emma was not a particularly affluent young lady. She was probably somewhere around 18 or 19 years old at the beginning of the war and was doing odd jobs to make ends meet. She struggled with her health and what appeared to be a broken family. The logistics of the letters, though, were important for gauging this. I noticed in the routing information that Emma, despite being on the "home front" sent her letters from a wide variety of post offices throughout southern Ohio. At one point I wondered if she even fit the geographic limitations of my dissertation research. But had she not included that routing information (and wise archivists including the envelopes at times), I would not have known about her transient status. In many ways knowing that seemingly small detail helped me better understand the rocky relationship between Emma and Edwin so I could contextualize it beyond just being in the midst of a terrible war.

As researchers move through a specific letter, it is important to jot down details that might help with historical context, but it is not always immediately evident what they mean. Write them down anyways. Those challenges, like with the example of Emma above, helped me realize that even though Emma moved around a good bit throughout the war, her letters to and from Edwin still arrived at their destinations. That gives historians a better understanding of the reliability of Civil War postal services as well as a new, more nuanced conception of romantic relationships during the war.

Chapter 2: Defining Historical Context

The difference between a historian and an antiquarian has everything to do with context. An antiquarian might be obsessed with the buttons on a jacket or the particular caliber of bullets in specific guns. However, a historian knows how to tell the story around those artifacts. A historian can define and describe the importance of all sorts of documents, artifacts, or even people as they relate to the larger narrative. Sometimes historians situate a piece of information in the midst of a local narrative, sometimes a national narrative, and sometimes a global narrative, but that ability to put a historical moment or source in its context is vital for the process of understanding the source itself. What soldiers wrote at different times and places in the midst of the Civil War directly influences how historians and readers should interpret the document. While the process is involved and may seem "off task" in pursuing secondary research, it really is an important element of the process of fully understanding a Civil War letter.

After the initial read through of a document as detailed in the opening chapter of this book, it is necessary for the researcher to review the information gained. What are some of the vital bits of information from the soldier and his family? Be sure to make note of unit affiliation, rank, and any locations found in the letter. Those are the signposts to guide further research. Although being in a particular unit does not necessarily guarantee that a soldier saw all of the same battles or events as that unit, but it does increase the likelihood.

Unit Affiliation

When a soldier expressed his military unit, he did so for practical reasons about getting mail and information to him. But there was much more in the identity of a unit because in the Civil War military units were still raised by local organizations. So, for example, a particular Civil War regiment would have nearly all soldiers from the same state. Then within the company (roughly 100 men), soldiers were often from neighboring counties. It did not mean that the men all "knew each other" as some have haphazardly asserted, but rather that local affiliations mattered to the men. Reputations were extremely important and influenced significant factors such as courage in battle or willingness to desert.

Unit affiliation also gives considerable insight into where individual soldiers were at different points in the war. Some soldiers loved to discuss physical

23

locations in great detail, but not all of them. Having the unit designation allows researchers to handle basic questions such as what campaigns the soldier most likely experienced, whether they were in the eastern or western theaters, and even the enlistment and discharge times. Each soldier's story is unique, but unit affiliations give great context to those stories.

In order to maximize information gleaned from these details, researchers would be wise to search for a *regimental history* for the unit. These can often be found through local or state-level libraries. Sometimes they are digitally available, but often they are massive old books that chronicle the events that a particular regiment saw through the war. Most regimental histories do not have much narrative, preferring instead to deliver essential details about each company, officer, and a full roster of names. Sometimes the rosters include information about transfers, wounds, awards, and the soldier's fate. These books can be an invaluable resource for understanding what type of uniform the soldier would have worn, weapon he would have carried, or even sometimes the food the soldier would have been fed.

While searching for regimental histories, researchers might also find works by historians about particular regiments. These works, more recent than regimental histories (typically written in the late 19th century), provide more depth of analysis than what most veterans groups wrote in earlier versions. More recent regimental histories often include a collection of sources. Historians call these developments of sources, "historiography," or put more simply the history of the history. Reading the historiography for a unit or even the larger "army" the soldier was a member of might help better understand the overarching conditions the soldier endured. Although it may not be all sources from the soldier whose letter you are researching, spending some time with sources from another soldier in the same unit can add depth of understanding to the letter in question. These books and articles by other historians are called secondary sources (as opposed to primary sources, which were written by people during the war, like the letter).

Rank

Not quite as valuable as unit affiliation but still important, knowing a soldier's rank helps researchers contextualize the soldier's work and experience. For example, a soldier who enlisted and discharged as a private did not have any increased responsibilities in the army. However, a soldier who rose through the ranks to sergeant would have done more and had more responsibilities. This might change an interpretation of a document considerably.

Determining whether a soldier was an officer or a "common soldier" (below the rank of captain), definitely alters the interpretation of the source. Officers and common soldiers experienced different things in the Civil War. Even "low level" officers had power and responsibilities that weighed heavily on them. On the other hand, they often carried with them benefits in terms of space, personal connections, and even the potential for wealth. Common soldiers, however, did not have much power or control and had to do the brunt of the heavy lifting. Common soldiers did not have the same responsibilities that officers had regarding logistics, battle command, and care for the troops.

Locations

If the researcher is fortunate enough to have several letters from a soldier and they all have locations on them, it is easy to develop a timeline of movement. But that often is not the case. If working with one specific letter, there may be a location given but it may not be easy to find on a map. When soldiers were in "enemy country" they were not always familiar with town names and exact locations, so they would use references like "about thirty miles west of Richmond," or "five miles north of the Tullahoma River." These bits of information were often the best a soldier could do to help his family and friends know where he was.

Following along with these locations, though, help researchers grasp potentially what a soldier's tasks were, whether or not they were in danger, and even infer the quality of life. Depending upon the chronological context, knowing where a soldier was serving could directly influence his work. Garrison duty sitting outside of Washington, D.C. guarding a train or entrenchments might not have been rigorous work. Then again, marching with the Army of the Potomac or the Army of Northern Virginia might have meant a considerable amount of foot sore, war weary men. Sometimes remote locations like western Virginia, most of Kentucky, or the border states of the west meant hard fighting among guerrilla forces, even though those battles tend not to make the general overviews of the Civil War. It is easy to assume that soldiers who were not at Gettysburg or Antietam experienced little combat. This is not the case, as many of these soldiers endured a considerable amount of fighting during the war.

Chronology

The most immediately important detail for analyzing and contextualizing a Civil War letter is chronology. Find out when the letter was written. Then, using that information, figure out what was going on in the context of the war. Where were the big battles? Who was governor of the state? When was it in relationship to important turning points like the Emancipation Proclamation, Gettysburg, or the emergence of trench warfare at Petersburg. Was the writer experiencing the siege in Vicksburg or the open-field combat in central Pennsylvania? Knowing dates can really help with these other context clues.

The easiest way to chronologically contextualize the source is to plot the date amidst other important events. A general survey of the Civil War could do this, but even a localized history of the war from a state level could work. Take a look at the tone of the letter as it connected with chronology. Did the soldier seem exhausted from fighting? marching? Were they eager to see combat, or had seen enough? Were they lamenting heading back home after a long war, or eager to meet the enemy in the early war? These types of comments even from the tone of a letter can help readers get a grasp on what the soldier was really trying to say beyond the words on the page.

Where historical context exists to help the researcher better understand the source, seeking corroborating evidence has a bit more of a cynical side to it. Here the researcher has to distrust the letter writer just a little bit and figure out if the source is credible. There are not many "fake" Civil War letters out there (merely because genuine sources are so numerous that forgeries are not terribly valuable), so it is not about spotting a forgery so much as figuring out if the soldier knew what he was writing. It might seem a bit condescending to disbelieve someone so many years later, but it is important for giving the letter a fair read. Corroboration involves using formal and reliable research to determine which elements of the letter are credible and which are not.

Every soldier and citizen was a part of something larger than him or herself, even if they did not readily admit it in correspondence. For example, a woman on the home front who made food or clothing to send to her soldier was a part of a larger movement of home front support. Soldiers were evidently a part of their military unit, but may have also fit into other larger social movements like a particular Christian denomination, a social organization like the Freemasons, or even in an unofficial category of people such as those "wounded in action" or even type of service. Corroborating accounts with others in similar categories can help the researcher learn more about the letters in question. It can also create a much stronger analysis of the document itself by connecting to others with similar experiences.

There are literally thousands of Civil War related material released every year. The most important and timeless reference materials are the Official Records of the War of the Rebellion, now available free online. It was originally collected in the 1880s in the wake of the Civil War. Some historians are critical of the sources, reporting that sometimes officers changed the events of a particular battle or campaign to protect the reputations of some other soldiers. However, every regimental history and most respected military accounts rely upon the Official Records (OR) for necessary details to corroborate the experiences of individual soldiers.

The best place to locate all available sources on a particular soldier's experience is at the National Archives and Records Administration (NARA) in Washington, D.C. Specifically for the Civil War, NARA has the pension records for Union soldiers. There historians can find the full official pension file for a specific soldier. Many soldiers applied for a pension after the war, providing documentation to justify coverage. Sometimes it included grim details about the after effects of war, such as injuries that hindered a man's ability to work. These pension records often included accounts from other soldiers about the soldier's service, including many minor details of his service. In addition to military detail, pension records sometimes included social history information about occupations or relationships because wives often applied for pensions on their husband's behalf and had to provide proof of marriage. As a side note, check the pension record whether or not the soldier survived the war; survivors often requested pensions based on partial disability (even if they were not necessarily wounded in battle) and the living associates of those who died requested pensions, thereby leaving details on the soldier's life.

So how does someone go about getting a pension record from the National Archives? First of all, it is best to do some research through the National Archives online to ensure that you have enough information on the soldier. If you have a version of the name and a unit affiliation, it is a good idea to find the soldier on one of numerous indexing websites that have the microfilm roll number. Consider beginning your search with the National Archives' suite of tools: https://www.archives.gov/research/start/online-tools.html. Then, when arriving at the National Archives, you will already know what roll you are seeking. Be sure to arrive early and have more time than you think you will need. There are only a few pull times throughout the day, so getting there early is key. Once there, ask one of the expert archivists behind the desk to show you how to fill out a pull slip.

Fill it out and wait to receive the pension record. Once you have it, quickly skim it to make sure that you found the right soldier. Once you are sure that you have the right soldier, copy the entire file. It will pay off in the end to have it available for review. In fact, it might be worthwhile to explore each document in the pension file much like the steps given in chapter two on historical context.

Of course if a researcher is not able or willing to travel to the nation's capitol for research, the NARA has research services available. For only one pension record (as opposed to a full research project on many soldiers), it may indeed be more economically feasible to buy copies of the file. It is no less scholarly to attain the research this way and may indeed be the best method for many researchers. However, anyone pursuing this research for graduate school or beyond is advised to set foot in the National Archives themselves. They are breathtaking for historically-minded folks.

Some sources other than pension records available at the National Archives include the daily log book for particular regiments. This is some of the most minute information available, showing who was present and accounted for at roll call, various tasks, and of course more significant records of combat. It can be the perfect corroborating evidence, though, when determining the minor details of a particular letter. Oftentimes when historians are looking at several soldiers over a long period of time, they do not take the time to study this level of detail. But there is certainly much to learn about a soldier in the days up to and following the letter in question. This corroborating evidence is key.

There are many examples I could give when it comes to historical context, but one of the most important was a series of notes from a young lady named Fannie Ford. She wrote letters to her uncle who was off at war, explaining that she was encountering rebel soldiers in southern Ohio. Initially I did not follow what she was talking about. Rebels in Ohio? What on earth was she talking about? As I read more into the letter, Ford mentioned how she felt feeding bread to these Confederate soldiers. As she talked about their appearance and the amount of dust their horses kicked up, I couldn't help but think about what a difficult letter that would have been for her uncle to read. After a bit of corroborating research, I soon found that she was referencing Confederate raider John Hunt Morgan's raid in the summer of 1863. While I utilized the account to make a point about the connection between the home and battle fronts, the account was a difficult challenge in corroboration and context. After learning about the larger context of Morgan's Raid, I was better able to understand Ms. Ford's story and why she felt so pressed to convey the experience to her uncle. It was a fascinating account made only more clear and interesting through the additional historical context research of connecting Ford to the larger narrative.

If I had only taken Ford at her word, it may have been impossible to connect her story to something larger. But instead, I utilized the dates and other secondary research to reconstruct what was happening in that iconic summer. As I worked to make those connections, I realized that there was a lot of "reading between the lines" that has to happen with historical research. Sometimes the researcher has to imagine the narrative in places where it is patchy or even inaccurate.

Chapter 3: Reading Between the Lines

One of the hardest parts in the process of historical research is figuring out what soldiers meant when they wrote particular passages. Oftentimes soldiers were writing to a specific person in context, so our reading of it out of that context can seem very unclear. This is where a bit of historical creative thinking helps researchers get a better grasp of what the letter really means and the message it really carried with it.

All of the points of historical context mentioned earlier become relevant with reading between the lines. For example, knowing the addressee of a letter might allow for a bit of investigative reading, such as if a soldier wrote home to his children or to his mother. Some men chose to tell their mothers gory detail about the gruesomeness of the war, but many chose to edit that part out of their letters. The tone and style of a letter to a soldier's father might take on masculine coded language about honor or courage, as often fathers expected of their sons. Similarly, letters that were intended for the whole community to read have much less personal information and much more detail of general interest. Letters to be published in the local newspaper tended to summarize overall "news from the front" rather than the specifics of one soldier's experience.

Another way to read between the lines beyond audience is structure. When soldiers found themselves in unique circumstances those often influenced the type of writing. So, for example, what kind of stationery is the letter on? What type of location does the soldier explain in the letter, if any? If the soldier is in a camp in a relatively "safe" location, there might be stationary from the Christian Commission or other types of obvious ways that outsiders supported the soldier. However, on the front, soldiers might write on smaller pieces of paper, scribble in the margins, or even write cross thatch to try to send more words home for the limited space. These are all "between the lines" context clues that help inform the mood, situation, and overall quality of life for the soldier. Grasping a sense of the tone, then - such as panic, joy, fear, happiness, and so on - allows the letter reader to have a clue as to what some of the other messages in the letter might mean.

Another method of reading between the lines involves decoding messages that were culturally coded for the Civil War era. Soldiers and their families sometimes used phrases that seem strange or unfamiliar to us. For example, folks in the north used a term "seceshers" when discussing southerners. This word does not appear in any dictionary and might seem totally unknown, but it was a derisive shortened form of "secessionists." Nineteenth century Americans sometimes used terms like this because they were not necessarily well educated, but sometimes they used it for a little bit of fun, too.

It is important for readers to seek to understand a wide range of emotions presented in letters. It is not uncommon for a letter to contain fear, dread, anxiety, frustration, anger, love, homesickness, joy, and humor all at different points in the writing. If we use the modern equivalent of a phone conversation or video call with a friend or loved one, we can expect to find a variety of emotions. Without the advantage of verbal or visual cues, the only way researchers have to determine the letter's message are the words themselves. Seek out the inflections in the words. Nineteenth century writers tended not to use the emotive cues common in 21st century writing such as "haha" or "lol." Because of this, researchers need to piece together the context of a comment to determine humor, sarcasm, or teasing. But please remember that not every letter written in wartime has to hold a deep sense of fear, dread, or impending death. These were human beings experiencing the full range of human emotions in their lives, including in their writing.

However, allow the emotional gravity of a sad or sorrowful letter to influence you as a researcher. Do not be so cool as to turn off an emotive response to a letter. The power of empathy and sympathy allow researchers to transcend the immediate reaction of the source and connect more deeply with its writer and audience. Ask yourself, "how would I feel if..." Be sure to connect with multiple characters in the scenario in an effort to get a fuller picture. This is an integral part of reading between the lines because it fills the emotional space that writing leaves. The words on the page can depict real concrete things, but often the letters were full of seemingly mundane information in an effort to essentially be together as correspondents. Not every face to face conversation is full of compelling insights. That is why many times letter writers wrote about ordinary events in their lives, so that when these deep emotional moments about a comrade's death or something awful observed in the midst of combat, the letter still provided an appropriate place for the account to dwell.

The heart of emotion in Civil War letters focused primarily on the relationships between people. Although political situations obviously created emotional responses, more often than not impassioned letters had relationships at their core. In that regard, researchers would be wise to try to "read between the lines" of those relationships. Are they strained? How is the marriage? Are the parents scolding or comforting? Is the soldier responding to rumors or accusations? These types of questions might seem a bit more like a psychologist's work than a historian's, but they are the questions that allow the letter to speak beyond simplistic detail. While it is interesting to know what a soldier ate for dinner or what the weather was like in the spring of 1863, it is oftentimes more important to grasping the totality of the war's experience to understand how the relationships evolved as a result of the cost of war. When historians only allow body count to determine the significance of war, there is a devaluation of life itself. Embracing the emotional and relational elements to these people allows researchers to bring them to life in far more profound ways.

Taking into account nuances like humor or sorrow, researchers must also put on a bit of a critical eye while reading between the lines. Just because it is on the page does not mean it is right. Letter writers often reported things that were unconfirmed or mere rumors. They, of course, did not realize they were essentially spreading falsehoods. This is why it should be considered reading between the lines. A researcher should not be looking to prove the account false to discredit it. Rather, the researcher should seek out corroboration from other sources for what was reported in the letters. For example, if an account reports that a soldier "will be coming home in a few weeks" and there are no other letters in the collection, do not assume that soldier's prediction came true. Use the service record of the unit or some other source to confirm. There are often significant sections of time completely absent from historical narratives. If that is the case with this soldier's account, perhaps it is safe to assume that he was correct. However, many times soldiers reported the end of the year, a pending big battle, or the always-appealing furlough trip home, but seldom did those events happen accurate to the prediction. Another way to think of the situation might be to ask the rhetorical question, "oh really?" as you read a letter. That skeptical tone as a reader will help the researcher attain information to be analyzed at a later date.

One of the great fears that researchers, especially amateur researchers, tend to have is a fear that they will "get it wrong." Push that out of your head for the reading between the lines part of historical interpretation. Historians argue over documents' meanings all the time. In fact, it is part of the process to present narratives and interpretations that disagree with one another. Not every reading of a particular source necessarily yields the same response or information gained, either. Maybe in the first read through of a letter the emotional response hit the reader deeply, but on the second or third reading the researcher picked up some military detail that gives a better sense of the soldier's actual job in his unit. Both readings are equally important in unlocking the wide variety of information available in a Civil War letter.

Perhaps the most moving example of "reading between the lines" that occurred for me in my research was the story of Van Brown of Athens, Ohio. He was the much-loved, humorous, and lively son of Almyra and William Brown. His letters between he and his parents, as well as occasionally his brother Edwin, revealed a young man with charisma and charm. As I read through his collection I literally laughed at his comments (including one chastising his mother for writing too often about delicious food back home) and found him to be amiable.

Later in the war the tone of Van Brown's writing was still positive, but the frequency slowed a bit. One letter to his parents included a comment about how he wasn't feeling well and that he planned to visit the doctor. The next letter his parents received was from his commanding officer, informing them of

Van's untimely death. He died a torturous death as a result of an affliction he contracted in the midst of war. His parents must have been devastated. His brother found out also in the form of a letter. Imagine his shock and sorrow.

But the real research story came a bit later, not from the initial news of death. After all, death is expected in the context of war. Rather, it was the very public expression of grief that followed in letters. Edwin, Van's brother, expressed that he supposed his mother would "never be the same." There were other comments, such as desiring the details of his death, that explained the deep humanity of the Brown family as they coped with their son and brother's passing. It was these details, nestled in the midst of what would have been just another "statistic" in a macro study of the war, that really drew me further into the story of the Civil War in southeastern Ohio. Using my tools of empathy and concern for the past, I was able to read between the lines to connect with the grief of a family from one hundred and fifty years ago. It is not easy work, but it is worthy work.

Chapter 4: Making Sources Available

So you have done all of the work to study a Civil War letter, so what to do with it now? Make it available to others. Provide the transcription and interpretation for other researchers. In a world of increased digital access to millions of pages of material, providing access to sources from the 19th century may seem completely unnecessary. However, increasing access to the sources improves historical study, helps to curb ignorance among others, and most importantly makes sure that the work of transcription and interpretation is available for posterity. There are primarily three ways to make the work available to others: traditional publication, online publication, and public donation. All of the options can be right for a particular situation, but that must be handle on a case by case basis.

Traditional publication probably would not happen with a single or a few sources, but scholars often edit and collect a variety of sources on a theme or topic. So, for example, having one letter from an Ohio Civil War soldier may not be enough to publish as a stand alone article, but a historian may analyze a collection of sources from a single county or region.

However, if the researcher has access to an entire unpublished collection, it may be worth pursuing traditional publication. Oftentimes academic presses prefer that a historian provide historical analysis via an introduction and other short form entries throughout the book. But amateur historians pursue this as well. Because Civil War letters are out of copyright, they are relatively easy to publish with a traditional press and Civil War topics are generally of interest to publishers. It would not be a simple pursuit, but it is one that would allow the collection to see the light of day beyond your eyes. If you use the methods presented in this book to analyze an entire collection of twenty, thirty, or more letters, there could realistically exist an excellent publication opportunity and a substantive contribution to our collective understanding of the Civil War.

Online publication is both easier and more complicated all at once. Publishing information on the Internet is easier now that it has ever been in history. A person can literally start a free webpage through a free web hosting service and within a few minutes have new, original content posted online. So you could start a new website for the sources that you have and post them online. Without marketing or site management, the letters posted would surely die in the obscurity of the Internet's recesses. That is obviously not a desirable outcome. Instead, it would be wise to connect the letters to other collections of Civil War sources, or, in a similar vein, post the letters to a site of Civil War collections. Sites like Civil War Archive (www.civilwararchive.com) or even submission threads on the popular site Reddit (www.reddit.com) allow people to submit sources. This might be one way to get the sources available to others. However, the best way to ensure that the sources will be properly indexed and available to scholars all over the world is to go through a professional archive, either at the local, state, or academic level.

Perhaps the best option is to donate the letter or collection to a university library or archive so that it can be properly indexed. Professional archivists not only know how to maintain sources (especially originals), they also know how to manage collections in a way that will provide access for other scholars. Even when government or university archives put sources online they tend to be more credible than those submitted by an amateur. Historians know that a trained professional vetted the documents before putting them online if it is associated with an archive, but that may not be the case with any random posting on the Internet.

The process of donating a source to an archive can be relatively simple, but the first decision is where to send the source. Consider how much location might matter. For research on southeastern Ohio, there are impressive collections at places like Ohio University and Marietta College in the region, but there are others housed at the state capitol in Columbus. Consider how well staffed the archive is, how quickly they will be able to process the source and make it available, and if they seem like they will actively assist scholars in using the sources they have. Archivists tend to be one of two persuasions; they either want to protect sources from harm or they want to help researchers have access to the sources. Protectors often create processes to prevent research and writing on a particular set of sources. Those who increase access tend to be more helpful to historians, but might be perceived as being a bit more careless with the sources themselves. Deciding proximity and type of archive is the first step, but after that point the process is unique to each archive. A quick phone call inquiring about the process of making a donation of original (or even transcribed) sources will yield the next steps. If the collection is perceived to be of value there may be an appraisal involved, but not always. Again, it depends on each specific archive.

Making sources available to other researchers and scholars is part of the responsibility of the historical professional and, by extension, even those who consider themselves amateurs. None of us owns the past and we have an opportunity to help others learn more. Of course we have a right to profit from our own work such as transcription and analysis, but we ought not restrict others from access to the sources themselves. Archives ought not restrict access to the materials that they have on hand or make memberships and fees so exorbitant as to prevent ordinary people from having access. Donating sources to publicly available archives, rather than for-profit archives, is desirable for making sure that, like state and national parks, historical sources remain freely accessible for posterity.

Because I do not own any of the sources used in my dissertation, I am unable to publish them as sources that stand alone. However, I have done my best to ensure that my research is publicly available through research libraries. Similarly, I included a breakdown of the letters for readers to seek out the sources for themselves. I found these types of publicly-available sources to be extremely helpful for my own research. Although it might seem important to keep the memory of your ancestors sacred, it can also be helpful to share it with researchers so that historians might better understand the past. The more collections of soldiers letters we have available for research, the better the research and conclusions can be for others.

Conclusion

This "how to" is intended to help the non-specialist make sense of a Civil War letter. Readers should be able to take a letter through from an initial read through to a useful interaction with the letter's historical value. Hopefully the process of studying and interpreting the letter's meaning provides a powerful, even transcendental time travel experience. But even if no real magic happens in understanding, there are enough practical skills in this book to help researchers at any level pick up a few helpful hints.

Some researchers find hurdles at the immediate level of trying to discern handwriting. Other researchers have no trouble reading the text, but have no idea what the words on the page actually mean. While others read the document, understand it, and have no idea how to situate it within a broader understanding of the Civil War. To be able to take all of these elements of the process and put them in a connected sense of what the letter means and why it matters - that is the point. It is a difficult, daunting, and unenviable process, but like most things "worth doing" after disciplining oneself to the research process, it can feel a bit like a Lazarean miracle.

Bringing a source back to life is enriching and, at times, thrilling.

One of the most exciting parts of reading and analyzing Civil War letters is engaging with people who have been long gone from this world. But they were equally human in their form and function during their lives as we are today. So taking the time to commune with them, to connect with them, and to learn about their deepest fears, concerns, and longings makes for a genuine, even soulful connection. This is where primary source research is so important for historians today. Sure, historians can read thousands of pages of writing from other scholars, but unlocking mysteries from seldom-examined sources like the letters of Civil War common soldiers adds a complexity to historical imagination that is not easily attained in another way.

I wrote at the beginning of the book that it is the book I wish I had when I started my research. Each step in the research and writing process presented new obstacles. You, too, will face obstacles along the way of your pursuit. But as you push forward using the instructions presented in this book, you will find that it can be a rewarding process. Making your way to archives or through portals that unlock the past can be invigorating. My journey took me through small local historical societies, through the esteemed halls of the Library of Congress, and into the depths of the National Archives, but some of the most important research I completed was on a laptop computer at my desk at home. Page after page of seemingly-ancient writing may hold the key to unlock the answers you need in your research. But sometimes, whether we like it or not, there's a database or a website with exactly the information necessary. Hopefully this book serves as a guide but also as an inspiration for others who desire to advance collective historical memory and research. It is my hope that others struggle less, or at least struggle differently, in a passionate pursuit of our shared and valuable past.

APPENDIX 1: Addresses

As discussed in Chapter 1, there are a number of different formats for addressing letters to soldiers and to the home front. This is an example of a letter sent from a soldier to his mother in Athens, Ohio. Note the simplicity of the information.

Image credit: Ohio University's Mahn Center, Athens, Ohio. Brown Family Collection Box 2, Folder 167.

APPENDIX 2: Script Transcription

There are, of course, as many types of handwriting as soldiers in the war. However, looking at a representative example might help readers when locating your own letters for transcription. Here is an excerpt from an original letter along with a brief transcription.

Image credit: Ohio University's Mahn Center, Athens, Ohio. Brown Family Collection Box 2, Folder 112.

"River that is 20 miles from Sommersville we camp in a big meddow thare Gen Ros[ecrans] had camp and had built a good Brest Works and 2 or 3 of our Boys Sleep in side of the Brest Works the Col Slep with us the Leut Col & Adjeant both slept thare I never saw the wind blow so hard in my life and cold two. we had with us a Teligraph Operator that night he sent a dispatch to Sutton and found out thare wasnt enny use of our going and that we was wanted more at home then thare so then..."

There are several points of note in this transcription, so let's break down a few of the key elements:

1) Punctuation was optional. - In the entire piece there is only one period.

2) Spelling was phonetic. - Editors will sometimes use the abbreviation *sic* to indicate an error on the part of the original author. For primary sources laden with so many errors, I prefer to leave it "as is." Although it can be difficult for readability, it preserves the tone and tenor of the   letter.

3) Context matters. - As you can see from my bracketed explanation of General Rosecrans, I had to do a little bit of contextual research for this letter. In order to discern which general the author was describing with the letters "Ros," I had to research the fact that General William S. Rosecrans was, in fact, in command of the mountain region of western Virginia in the early spring of 1862.

4) Who is Sutton? - As important as historical context is, there was no way for me to figure out who Sutton was. If I were to dig a little deeper in the research on the soldier's unit (Edwin Brown, 36th Ohio Volunteer Infantry), I might be able to identify someone further up the chain of command. But I chose not to pursue that for my particular research question. This is an important point for researchers, though. You cannot pursue every rabbit hole. Know your research limitations and make wise choices what to investigate.

5) And so it ends... - Soldiers were not big on conclusions to letters or paragraphs or ideas, so excerpting can be difficult. I just had to cut this one off. But editing Civil War letters can be a

tedious task. In transcription I preserve everything as I see it and only add when necessary and *always* use brackets if I touch the prose for readability and clarity.

APPENDIX 3: Letter Layout

Civil War soldiers had limited paper, so they often crammed as much as they could onto a letter. Today, most of us would start in the top left corner of the front of a page, write all the way down to the bottom, flip it over and repeat, with a salutation in the bottom of the back corner. Civil War soldiers followed a different formula, using a layout that accounted for the recipient opening the letter differently. Here's an example:

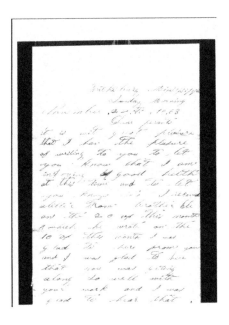

In this image, you can see the greeting in the top right side. This is actually the RIGHT side of a paper laying horizontal. It makes more sense as we continue.

This image shows page two and three of the letter. This is actually the "back" of the page, still laying horizontal.

This image is the final page. About two-thirds down the page is the salutation "good by to one and all." This is actually the LEFT side of the "front" of the letter. Even multi-page letters follow this similar layout.

-If you can imagine a soldier writing a letter and needing to fold it into a size smaller than a business envelope, this format makes sense. The page ends up one quarter its original size, making it easier for the soldier to carry before posting and simple to read when unfolded. The layout may be confusing to 21st century eyes, but it was quite common in 19th century sources.

Image credit: Courtesy of the Ohio Historical Connection, Columbus, Ohio, Coulson Family Papers, VFM 5567.

Bibliography

Cashin, Joan ed. *The War Was You and Me: Civilians in the American Civil War,* Princeton: Princeton University Press, 2002.

Cimbala, Paul. *Soldiers North and South: The Everyday Experiences of the Men Who Fought America's Civil War.* New York: Fordham University Press, 2010.

Hess, Earl J. *Liberty, Virtue, and Progress: Northerners and Their War for the Union.* New York: Fordham University Press, 1997.

--------. *The Union Soldier in Battle: Enduring the Ordeal of Combat.* Lawrence, Kansas: University Press of Kansas, 1997.

Scott, Sean A. *A Visitation of God: Northern Civilians Interpret the Civil War.* Oxford: Oxford University Press, 2012.

Sheehan-Dean, Aaron ed. *View from the Ground: Experiences of Civil War Soldiers.* Lexington, KY: University Press of Kentucky, 2007.

Silber, Nina and Mary Beth Sievens eds. *Yankee Correspondence: Civil War Letters between New England Soldiers and the Home Front.* Charlottesville: University Press of Virginia, 1996.

Acknowledgments

I am particularly indebted to a few friends and colleagues for their help. I am grateful to my friend David Harkleroad for his early consultation on the concept of the book. I am thankful to my mother, Patricia E. Jones, for her close read of the initial text. A special thanks goes to my grad school colleague and dear friend Chad Lower for his read of the manuscript. I am appreciative of his nudge to include more of my personality and experience, rather than keeping it a cool and detached methodology book.

I want to thank Tara Darazio, Brad Frey, Eric Miller, Adam Hodge, and Matt McDonough for their encouragement on this project. Without supportive people to keep me writing, I would not be able to complete this work. Special thanks also goes to Leonne Hudson, Lesley Gordon, Kevin Adams, Elizabeth Smith-Pryor, and Alexander Macaulay for their work as teachers in my own professional trajectory.

I am thankful to my readers. It is my hope that you found the book to be engaging and thoughtful. Hopefully, too, it solves some problems for you.

Lastly, I am thankful for the support of Jennifer Jones, my helpmate and best friend. It's a privilege to parent our children Sadie and Silas with her. I hope that some day they will appreciate the work that I do and the reason that I do it. After all, it is for the Glory of God alone that I pursue research and writing.

About the Author

Gregory R. Jones is a professional historian and teacher. He studies 19th century United States history with a special focus on Civil War soldiers and their connection with the home front. He is also interested in other veins of cultural history including sports and music history. He lives in Ohio with his wife Jennifer, daughter Sadie, and son Silas.